Come Follow
COLORING
BOOK FOR KIDS

AGES 1-5

THE BOOK OF MORMON

One coloring page & one drawing page for EVERY weekly
lesson for the ENTIRE year of 2024

ABOUT THIS BOOK

This coloring book is for kids ages 1-5. Each week has one coloring page and one drawing page to go along with the weekly Come, Follow Me lesson.

THIS BOOK BELONGS TO:

_____

LESSON SCHEDULE

January

Jan 1-7	Intro Pages
Jan 8-14	1 Nephi 1-5
Jan 15-21	1 Nephi 6-10
Jan 22-28	1 Nephi 11-15

February

Jan 29-Feb 4	1 Nephi 16-22
Feb 5-11	2 Nephi 1-2
Feb 12-18	2 Nephi 3-5
Feb 19-25	2 Nephi 6-10

March

Feb 26-Mar 3	2 Nephi 11-19
Mar 4-10	2 Nephi 20-25
Mar 11-17	2 Nephi 26-30
Mar 18-24	2 Nephi 31-33
Mar 25-31	Easter

April

April 1-7	Jacob 1-4
April 8-14	Jacob 5-7
April 15-21	Enos-Words Mormon
April 22-28	Mosiah 1-3

May

April 29-May 5	Mosiah 4-6
May 6-12	Mosiah 7-10
May 13-19	Mosiah 11-17
May 20-26	Mosiah 18-24

June

May 27-Jun 2	Mosiah 25-28
Jun 3-9	Mosiah 29-Alma 4
Jun 10-16	Alma 5-7
Jun 17-23	Alma 8-12
Jun 24-30	Alma 13-16

July

Jul 1-7	Alma 17-22
Jul 8-14	Alma 23-29
Jul 15-21	Alma 30-31
Jul 22-28	Alma 32-35

August

Jul 29-Aug 4	Alma 36-38
Aug 5-11	Alma 39-42
Aug 12-18	Alma 43-52
Aug 19-25	Alma 53-63

September

Aug 26-Sept 1	Helaman 1-6
Sept 2-8	Helaman 7-12
Sept 9-15	Helaman 13-16
Sept 16-22	3 Nephi 1-7
Sept 23-29	3 Nephi 8-11

October

Sept 30-Oct 6	3 Nephi 12-16
Oct 7-13	3 Nephi 17-19
Oct 14-20	3 Nephi 20-26
Oct 21-27	3 Nephi 27-4 Nephi

November

Oct 28-Nov 3	Mormon 1-6
Nov 4-10	Mormon 7-9
Nov 11-17	Ether 1-5
Nov 18-24	Ether 6-11

December

Nov 25-Dec 1	Ether 12-15
Dec 2-8	Moroni 1-6
Dec 9-15	Moroni 7-9
Dec 16-22	Moroni 10
Dec 23-29	Christmas

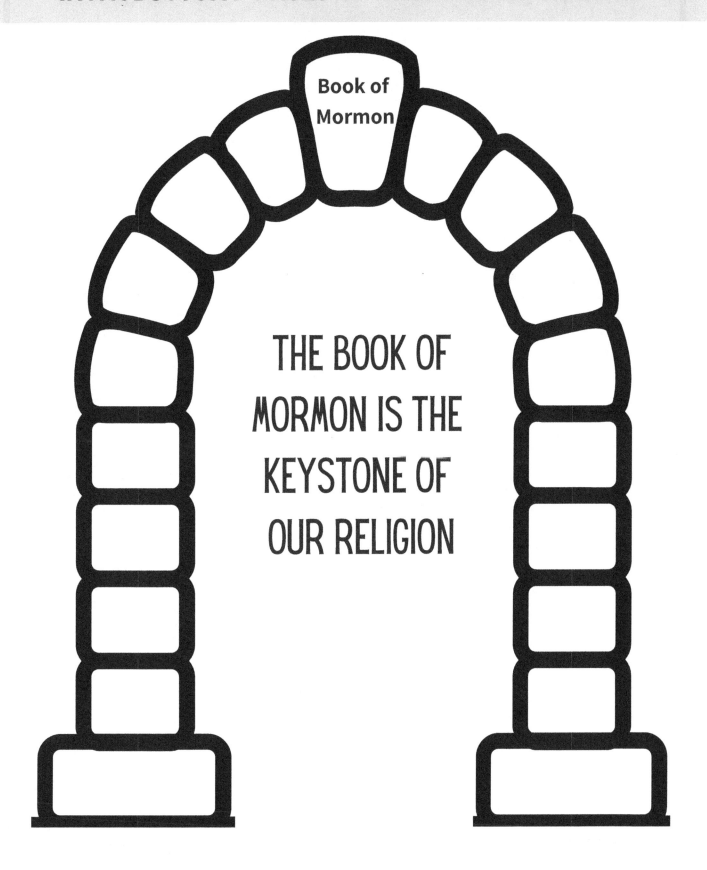

Book of Mormon

THE BOOK OF MORMON IS THE KEYSTONE OF OUR RELIGION

WEEKLY MASTERPIECE

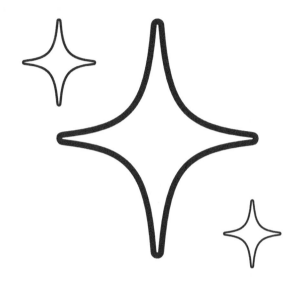

HEAVENLY FATHER
SENT JESUS
CHRIST BECAUSE
HE LOVES ME

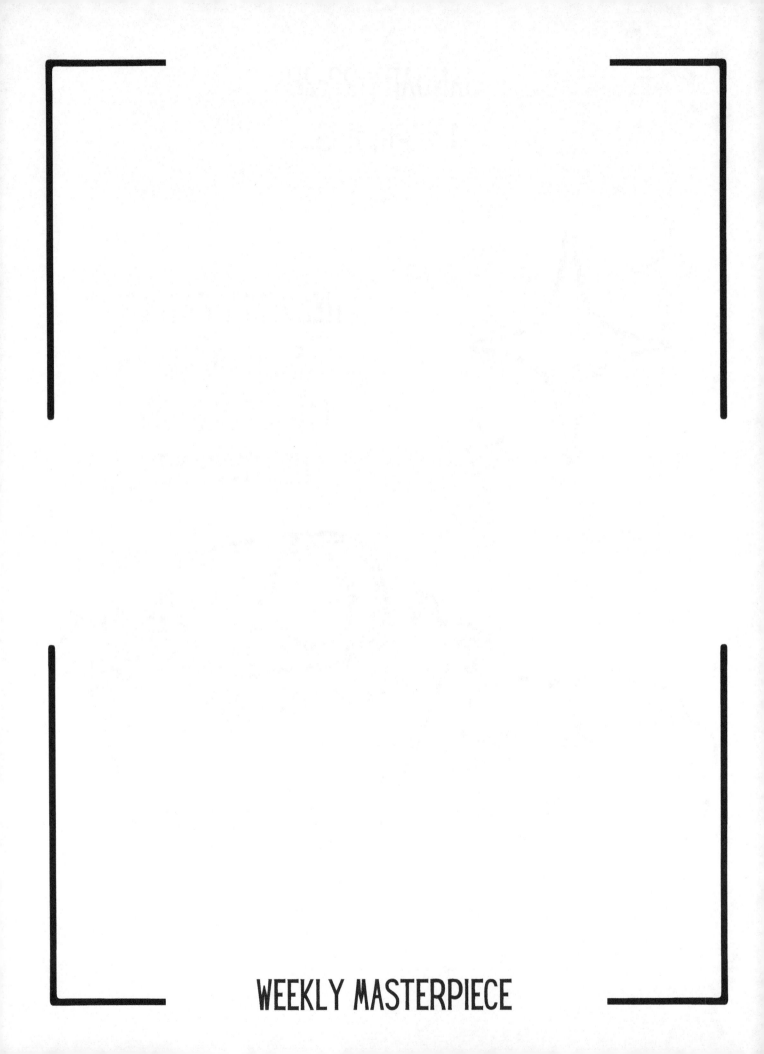

WEEKLY MASTERPIECE

JANUARY 29-FEBRUARY 4
1 NEPHI 16-22

NEPHI BUILT A BOAT

WEEKLY MASTERPIECE

I HAVE THE FREEDOM TO CHOOSE RIGHT OR WRONG

WEEKLY MASTERPIECE

HEAVENLY FATHER CALLS SEERS TO HELP US SEE THINGS WE CAN'T SEE

WEEKLY MASTERPIECE

FEBRUARY 19-25
2 NEPHI 6-10

"MY HEART DELIGHTETH IN RIGHTEOUSNESS"

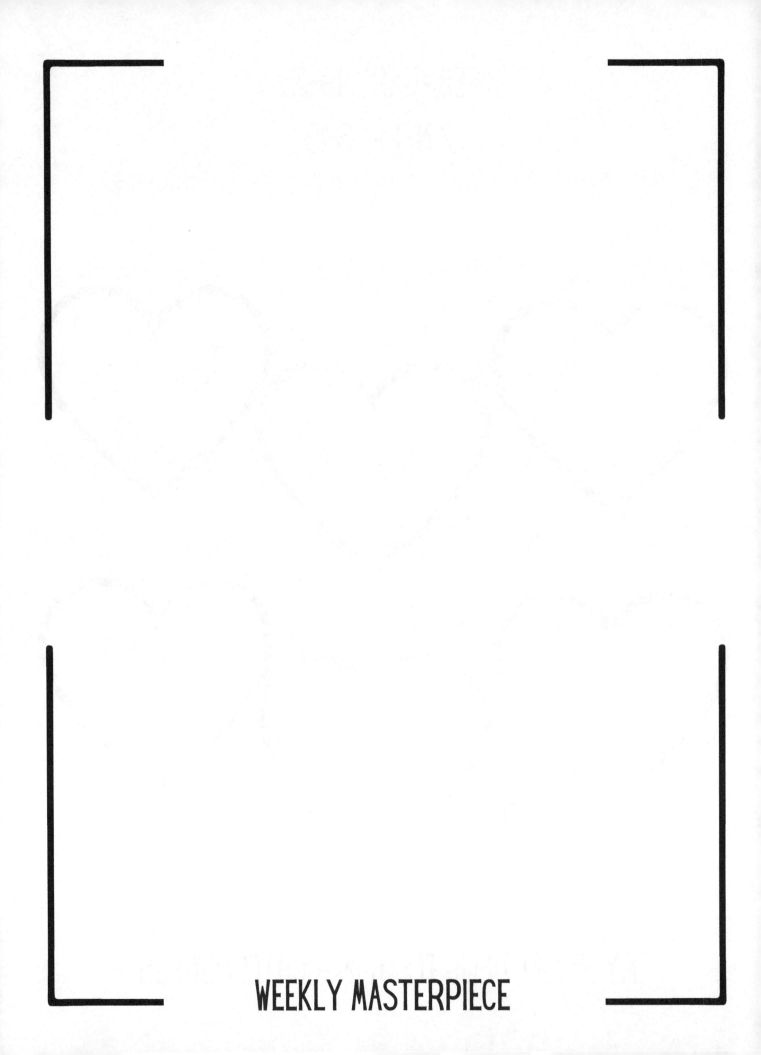

WEEKLY MASTERPIECE

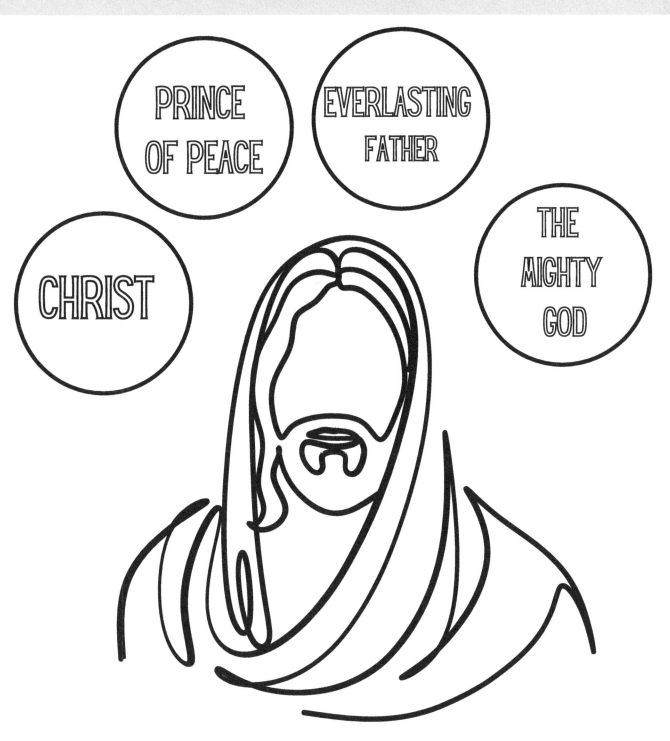

PRINCE OF PEACE

EVERLASTING FATHER

THE MIGHTY GOD

CHRIST

THROUGHOUT THE SCRIPTURES MANY NAMES OF JESUS ARE GIVEN

WEEKLY MASTERPIECE

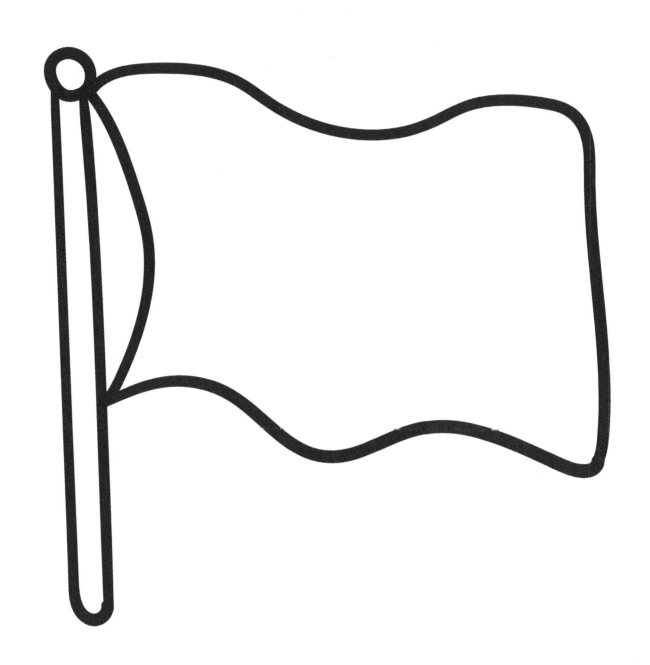

THE LORD IS GATHERING HIS PEOPLE & WILL SET UP AN ENSIGN FOR THE NATIONS

WEEKLY MASTERPIECE

THE

BOOK OF

MORMON

THE BOOK OF MORMON IS A GIFT & BLESSING TO ME

WEEKLY MASTERPIECE

JESUS TAUGHT US THE STEPS TO ETERNAL LIFE

WEEKLY MASTERPIECE

HE LIVES!

JESUS WAS RESURRECTED & I WILL BE, TOO

WEEKLY MASTERPIECE

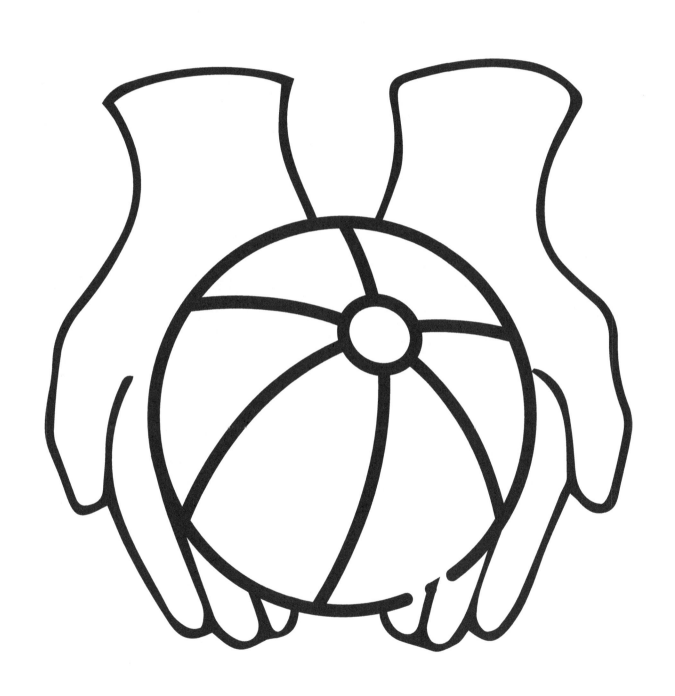

I CAN SHARE WITH OTHERS

WEEKLY MASTERPIECE

I LEARN FROM THE ALLEGORY OF THE OLIVE TREE THAT THE LORD CARES FOR HIS PEOPLE

WEEKLY MASTERPIECE

THINGS I CAN PRAY FOR

HEAVENLY FATHER HEARS & ANSWERS PRAYERS

WEEKLY MASTERPIECE

KING BENJAMIN TAUGHT IMPORTANT TRUTHS

WEEKLY MASTERPIECE

ACKNOWLEDGE WHAT YOU DID WAS WRONG

SAY "I'M SORRY" & FIX WHAT YOU DID

ASK HEAVENLY FATHER FOR FORGIVENESS

RECEIVE PEACE & FORGIVENESS. TRY YOUR BEST NOT TO REPEAT MISTAKE..

I CAN REPENT WHEN I MAKE A MISTAKE

WEEKLY MASTERPIECE

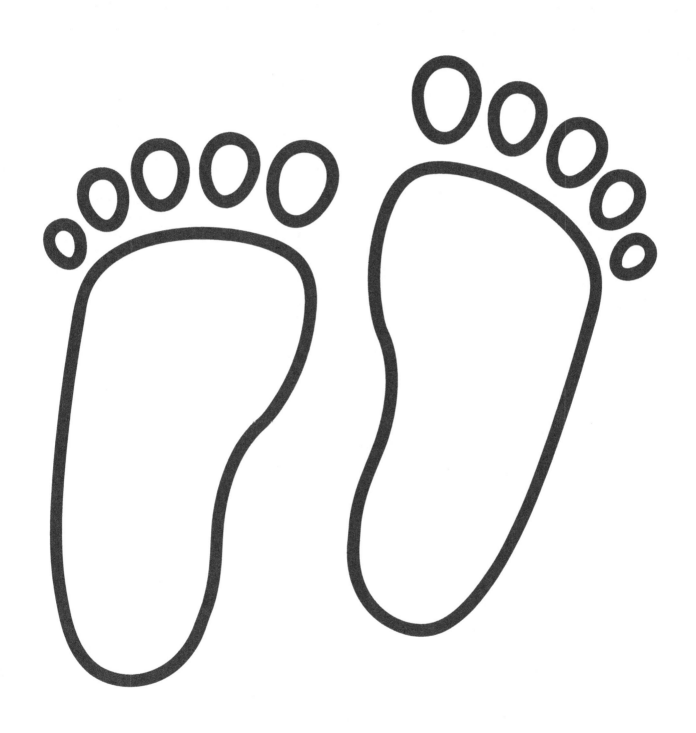

I WILL FOLLOW THE PROPHET

WEEKLY MASTERPIECE

ABINADI TAUGHT WE SHOULD OBEY GOD'S
COMMANDMENTS

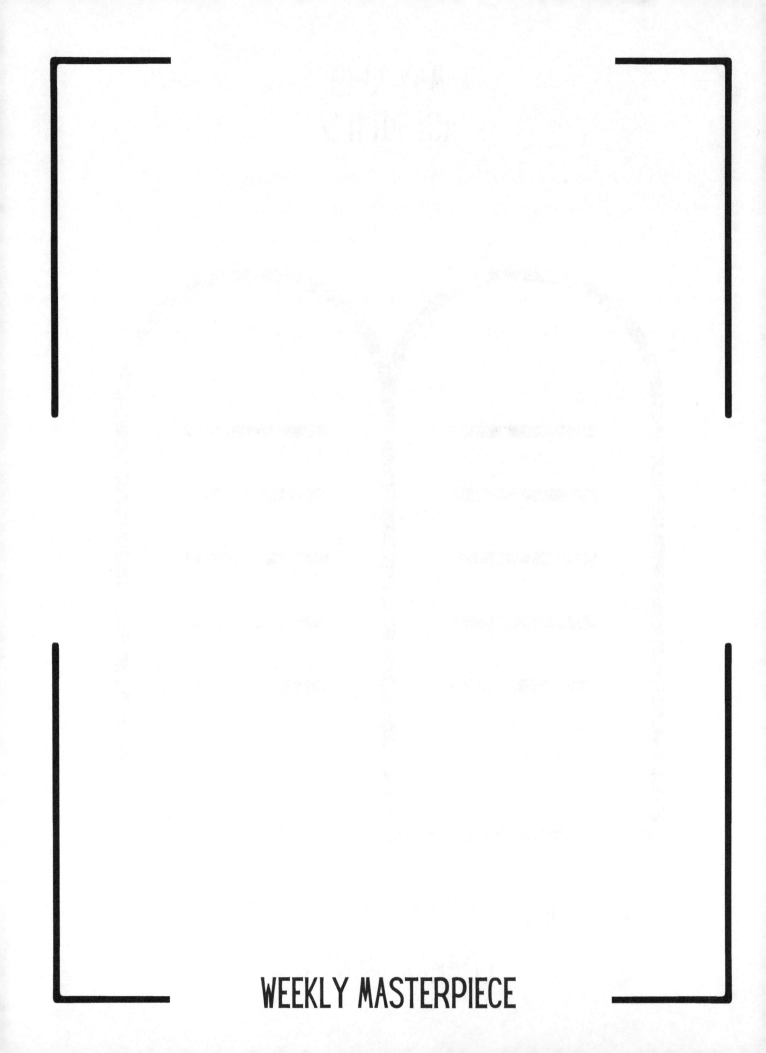

WEEKLY MASTERPIECE

WHEN WE ARE BAPTIZED, WE MAKE PROMISES TO GOD &
HE MAKES PROMISES TO US

WEEKLY MASTERPIECE

I CAN FAST AND PRAY FOR OTHERS

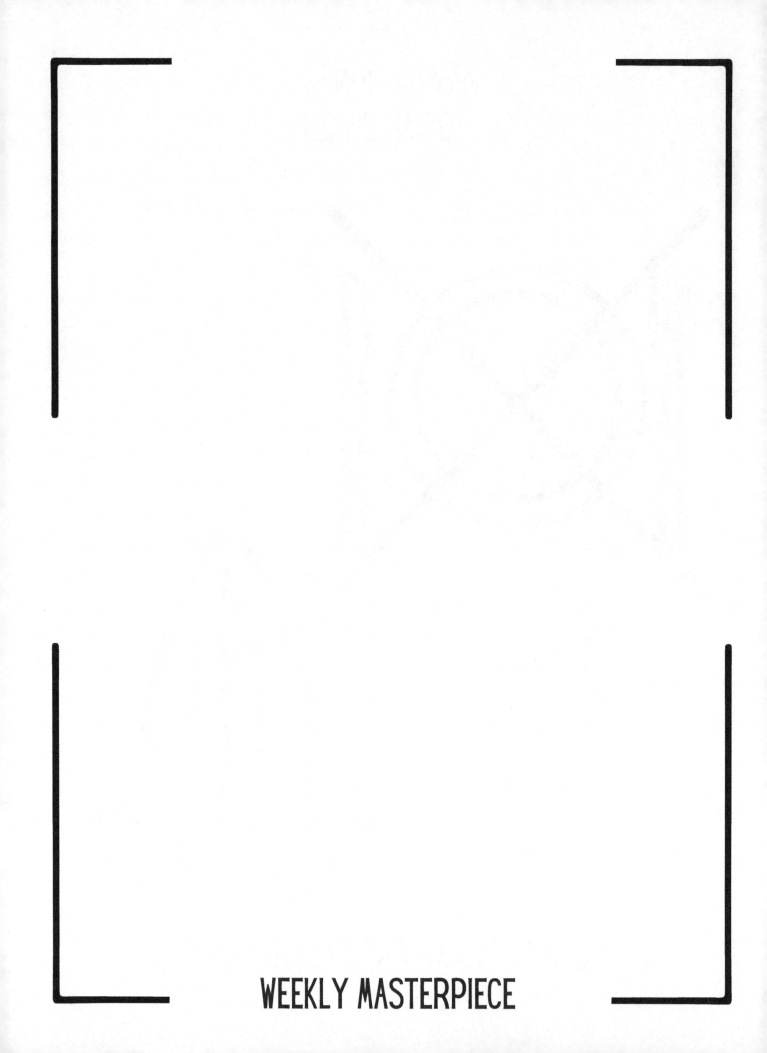

WEEKLY MASTERPIECE

A TESTIMONY IS LIKE A GARDEN

WEEKLY MASTERPIECE

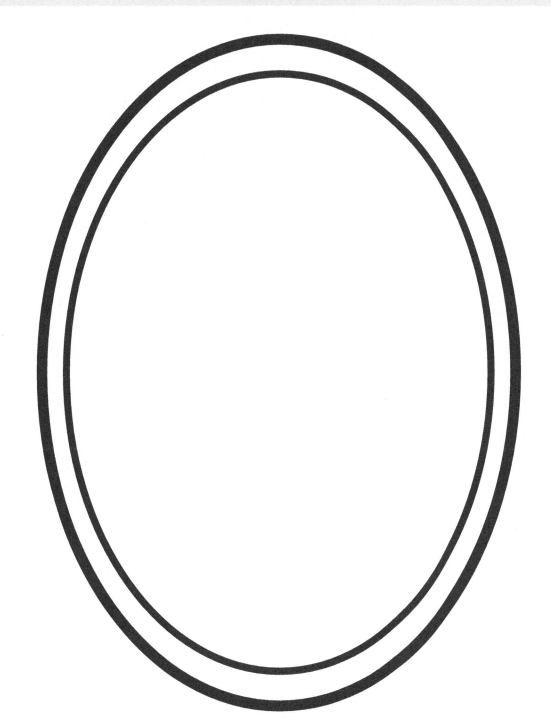

I CAN HAVE THE SAVIOR'S IMAGE IN MY COUNTENANCE
(COLOR A PICTURE OF YOURSELF IN THE MIRROR)

WEEKLY MASTERPIECE

I CAN BE A GOOD FRIEND

WEEKLY MASTERPIECE

THE LORD PROTECTED ALMA & AMULEK WHEN THE
PRISON FELL

WEEKLY MASTERPIECE

AMMON SAVED THE KING'S SHEEP

WEEKLY MASTERPIECE

THE ANTI-NEPHI-LEHIES MADE A PROMISE NEVER TO FIGHT AGAIN & BURIED THEIR WEAPONS

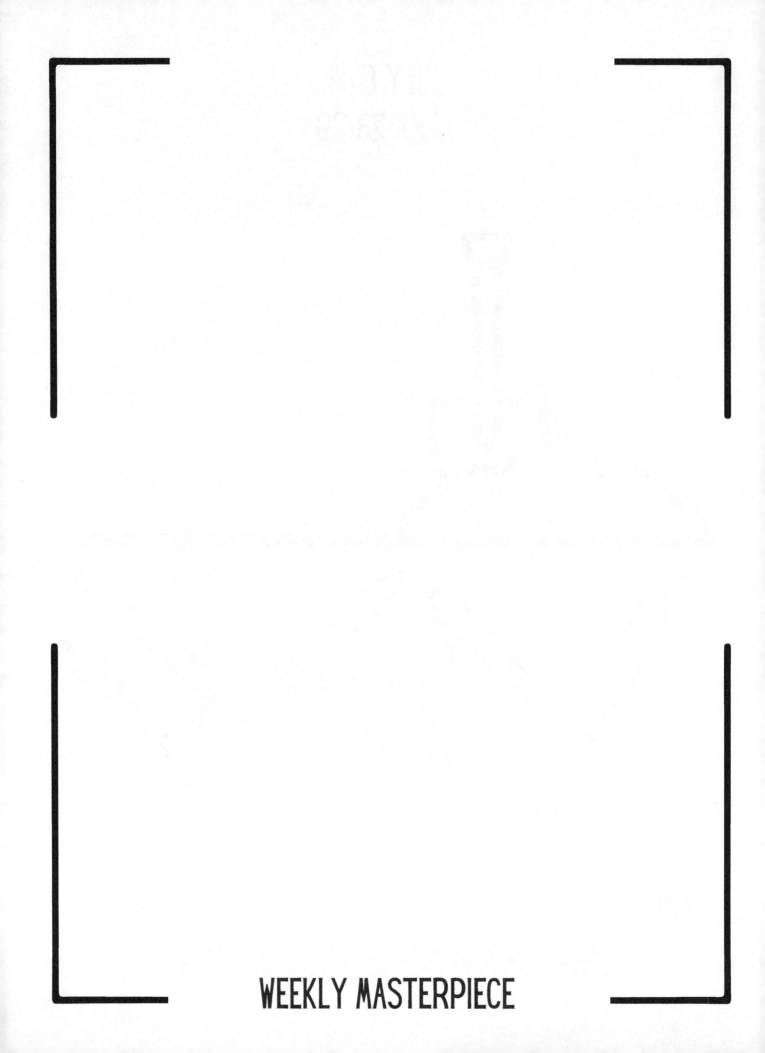

WEEKLY MASTERPIECE

HEAVENLY FATHER HEARS OUR PRAYERS

WEEKLY MASTERPIECE

MY TESTIMONY GROWS AS I NOURISH IT

WEEKLY MASTERPIECE

SMALL & SIMPLE THINGS CAN MAKE BIG THINGS HAPPEN

WEEKLY MASTERPIECE

SPIRIT WORLD

AFTER WE DIE, WE GO TO THE SPIRIT WORLD UNTIL WE ARE RESURRECTED

WEEKLY MASTERPIECE

WE CAN SPIRITUALLY PROTECT OUR HOMES

WEEKLY MASTERPIECE

I CAN BE FAITHFUL TO GOD LIKE THE STRIPLING WARRIORS

WEEKLY MASTERPIECE

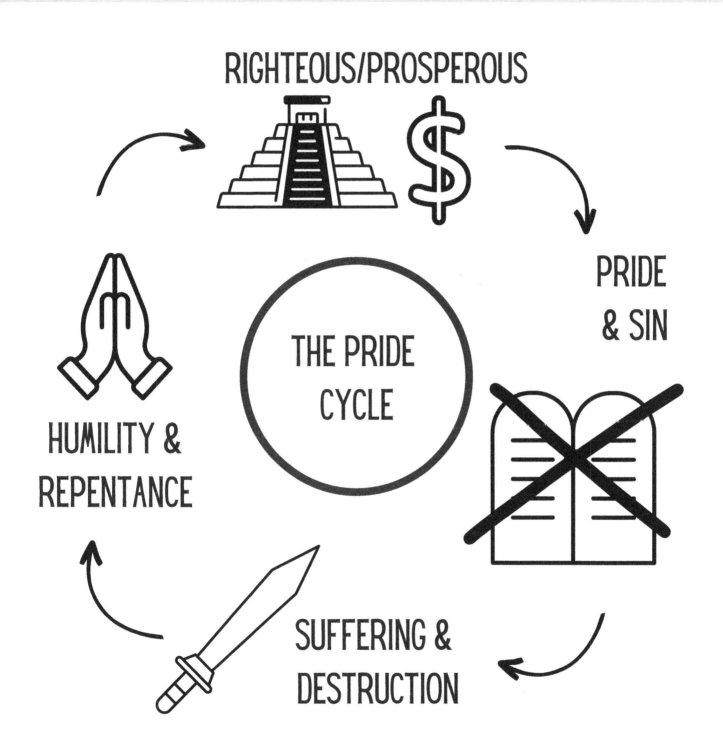

RIGHTEOUS/PROSPEROUS

PRIDE & SIN

THE PRIDE CYCLE

HUMILITY & REPENTANCE

SUFFERING & DESTRUCTION

GOD WANTS ME TO BE HUMBLE & NOT PRIDEFUL

WEEKLY MASTERPIECE

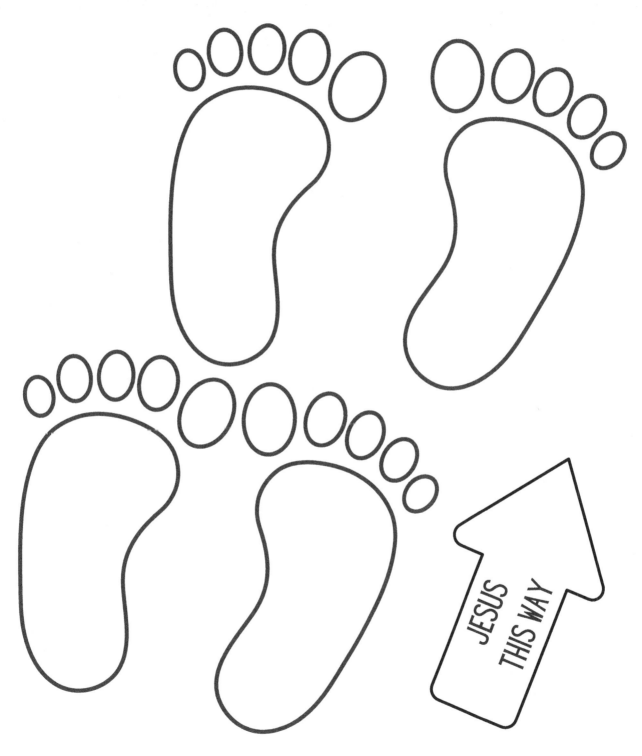

JESUS THIS WAY

PROPHETS TESTIFY OF CHRIST

WEEKLY MASTERPIECE

THOUGHTS THAT STAY ON YOUR MIND

SOMETHING YOU FEEL IN YOUR HEART

A WHISPER OR VOICE YOU HEAR IN YOUR MIND

A FEELING THAT YOU SHOULDN'T DO SOMETHING

A DESIRE TO FOLLOW THE COMMANDMENTS

A HAPPY, PEACEFUL FEELING THAT SOMETHING IS A GOOD CHOICE

GOD CAN SPEAK TO ME THROUGH THE HOLY GHOST

WEEKLY MASTERPIECE

THE NEPHITES SAW A NEW STAR APPEAR WHEN JESUS WAS BORN

WEEKLY MASTERPIECE

THERE WAS A GREAT STORM, FIRES, & 3 DAYS OF DARKNESS AFTER CHRIST DIED. THE RESURRECTED CHRIST VISITED THE NEPHITES.

WEEKLY MASTERPIECE

I WILL LET MY LIGHT SHINE

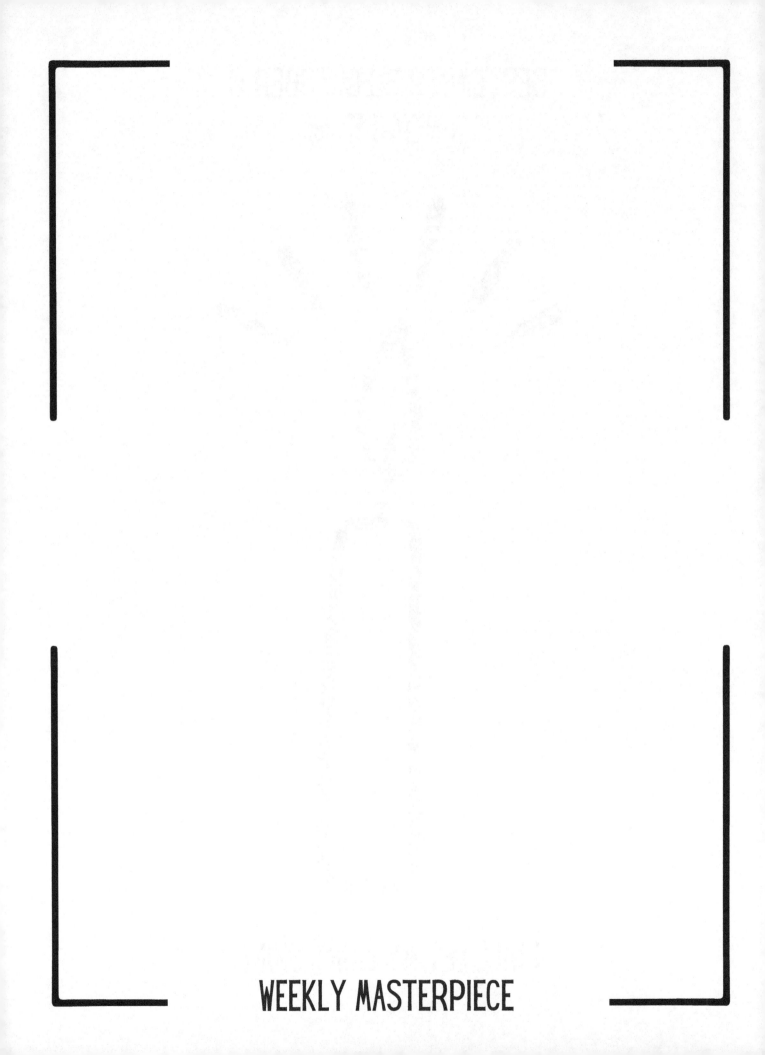

WEEKLY MASTERPIECE

ANGELS MINISTERED TO THE CHILDREN AFTER JESUS HAD BLESSED THEM

WEEKLY MASTERPIECE

FAMILIES CAN BE TOGETHER FOREVER

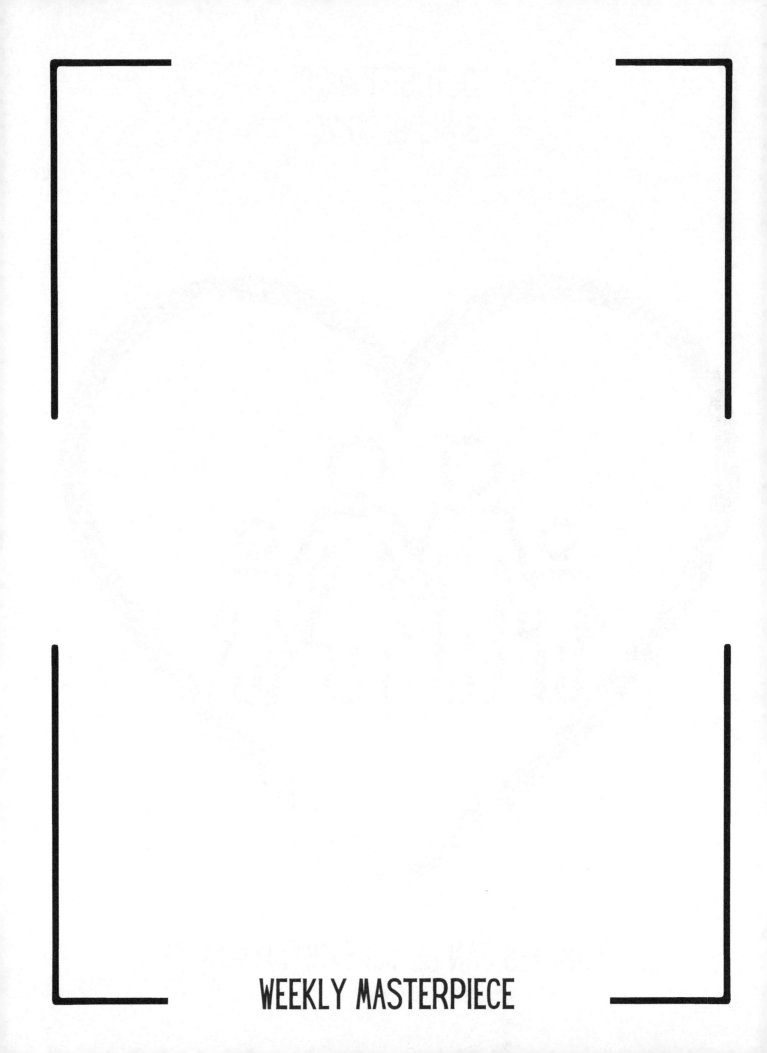

WEEKLY MASTERPIECE

I belong to the

# of Jesus Christ

WEEKLY MASTERPIECE

I AM GRATEFUL

DRAW THINGS ON THE LEAVES YOU ARE GRATEFUL FOR

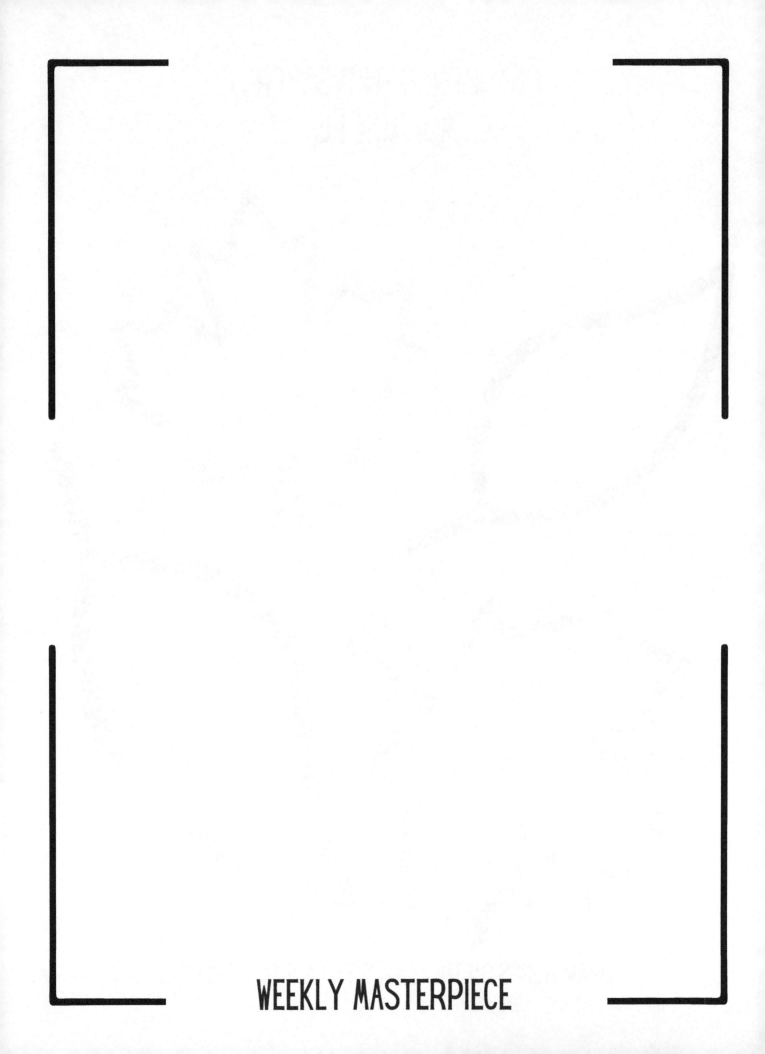

WEEKLY MASTERPIECE

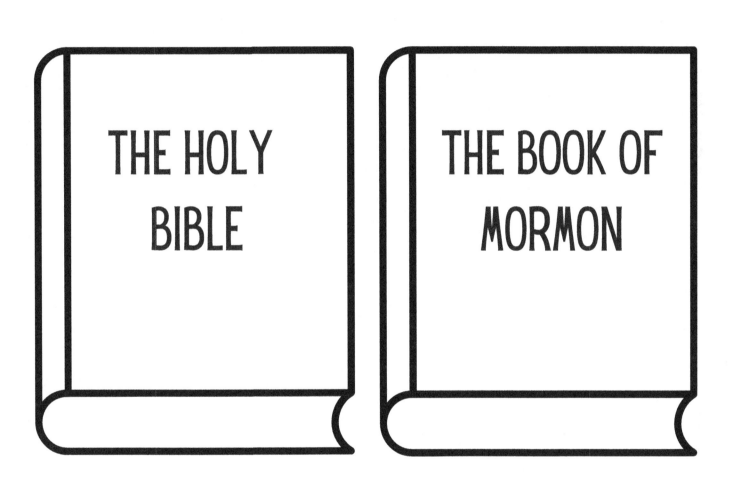

THE BOOK OF MORMON & BIBLE TESTIFY OF JESUS

WEEKLY MASTERPIECE

HEAVENLY FATHER ANSWERED THE JAREDITES PRAYERS & DID NOT CONFOUND THEIR LANGUAGE

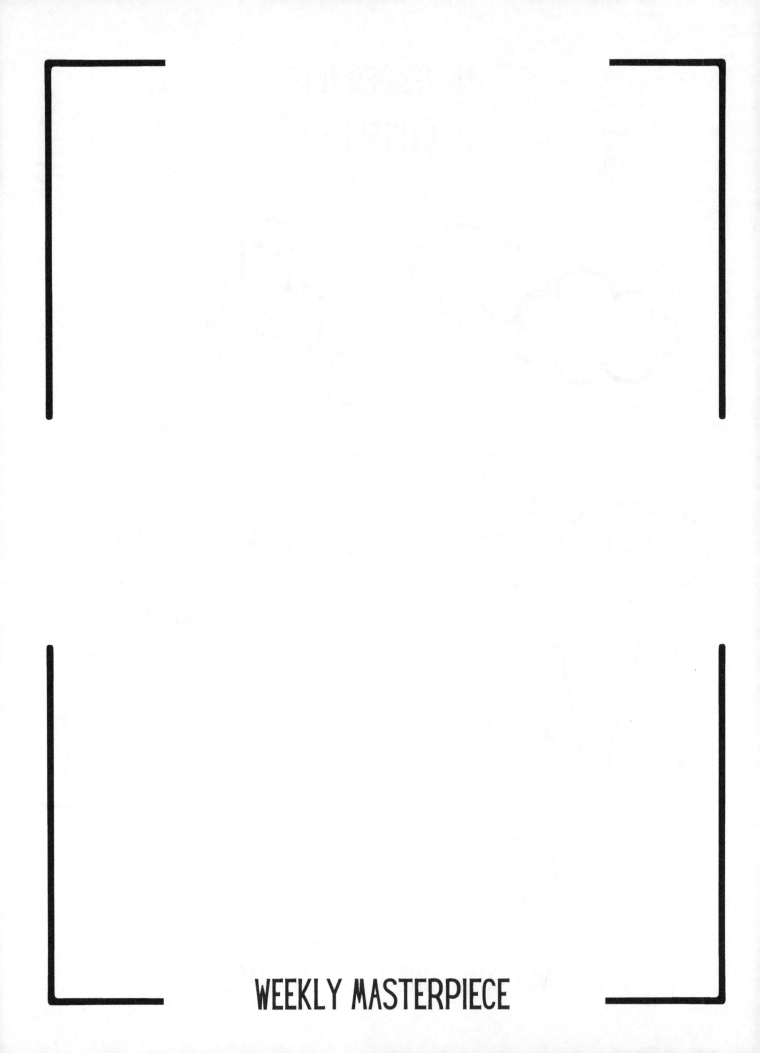

WEEKLY MASTERPIECE

THE LORD CAN COMFORT US WHEN WE ARE SCARED

WEEKLY MASTERPIECE

HOPE IS LIKE AN ANCHOR TO OUR SOULS

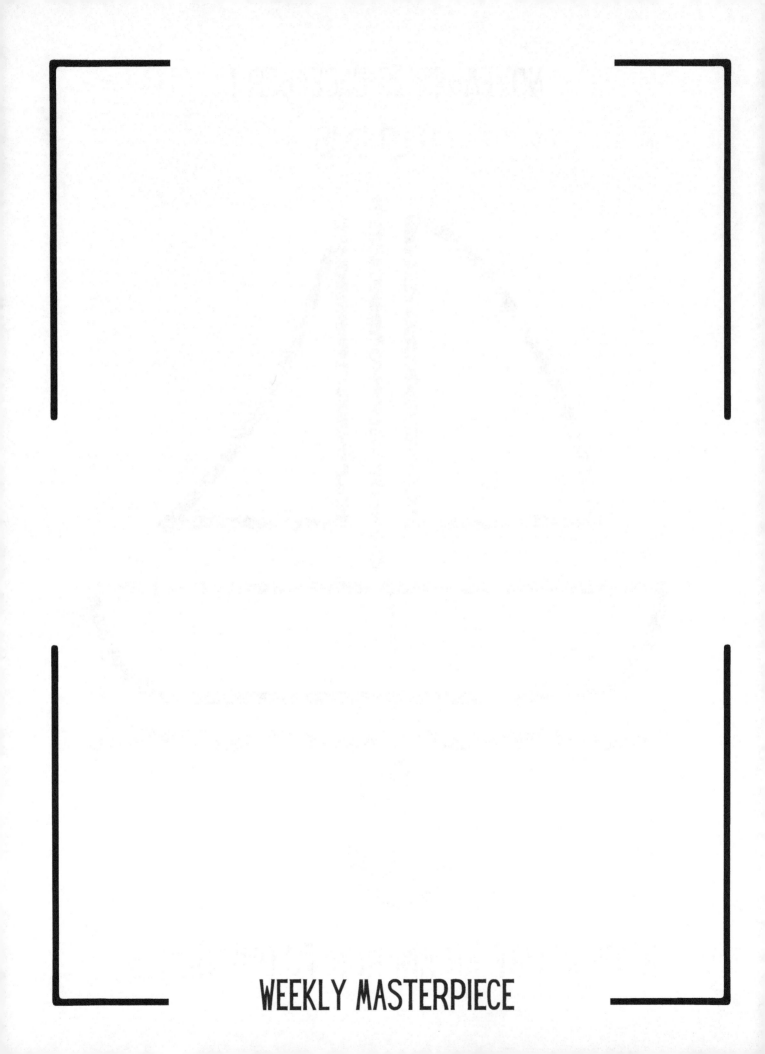

WEEKLY MASTERPIECE

JUST LIKE FRUITS & VEGETABLES CAN NOURISH US, WE CAN ALSO BE NOURISHED BY THE GOOD WORD OF GOD

WEEKLY MASTERPIECE

CHARITY IS THE PURE LOVE OF CHRIST

WEEKLY MASTERPIECE

I HAVE BEEN GIVEN SPIRITUAL GIFTS

WEEKLY MASTERPIECE

JESUS CHRIST CAME TO EARTH TO BE OUR SAVIOR

WEEKLY MASTERPIECE

IF YOU ENJOYED THIS BOOK, MAKE SURE TO LEAVE A REVIEW.

CHECK OUT OUR OTHER BOOKS.

FOLLOW US ONLINE!

@LATTER.DAY.DESIGNS

LATTER-DAY DESIGNS

Made in the USA
Las Vegas, NV
07 January 2024